Introduction

Dear Player,

By finding this personal training guide you have just taken the first step to becoming a better soccer player!

*I designed this guide to help **you** in the areas of player development that you can 'self coach' yourself on. Whether that is Improving your touch, getting quicker, or improving your conditioning or increasing your strength. All high level players are committed to improving their game outside of practice and matches. You need to develop a 'training mentality' to work on your game 5 days a week. The activities and exercises in this log will take you no more than 20 mins in most cases. All players of all levels of competition (Youth to Professional) can benefit from this manual. Listed below are the 3 main areas we need to improve or maintain as a player. These are our personal training goals........*

Goals of this **P**ersonal **T**raining **L**og;

There are 3 main goals for a player in their Personal Training:

1. **Technique** (Individual skills, 1 vs 1 skills, Touch)
2. **Fitness** (Aerobic, An-aerobic conditioning, Core & Functional)
3. **SAQ Training** (Speed, Agility, Quickness Training)

About this Skill & Fitness guide

This training program is for those players who are interested in improving their skill and fitness levels. Players who complete this additional training will show signs of improvement in the three areas discussed above.

Inside this manual you will see a number of skill and fitness training sheets which are color coded for a specific training goal. These codes are applied at different phases of the playing and off season as is shown in the chart on page 4. Each training code covers a seven day period and targets a sub-component of our 3 training goals highlighted above.

How your Training Log works

Each week if this is part of your academy program or team training your coach/director will assign you or the whole team one of the colored training 'codes'. If you are a single player assign your own codes using the chart on page 4 as your weekly reference. You should complete the activities to the best of your ability following the instructions and sign next to the activity indicating the exercise was completed. For younger players coaches may require you get your parents/guardians to sign in the box next to the activity so they can monitor your progress.

The Training Log as a workbook

Throughout the booklet you will see various symbols that are designed to make you think about a certain topic or help you organize your training. These are shown in the table below:

 Make a note

 Think for yourself

 Use these post-it notes to make your notes

 Important message for the author

Total Player Development

We are aiming to develop the 'complete player'. If you have completed this program, you will have increased your ability to perform football specific activities in the 3 areas highlighted. Sprint at a high intensity, recover and repeat it. Perform low intensity activities, jogging and cruising for longer periods. Have improved your quickness and multi-directional agility. By doing the functional work and regular bodyweight circuits you will have improved the strength and endurance of the specific football relevant muscles. Plus, you have also have improved your technical abilities with the ball by performing the skill codes!

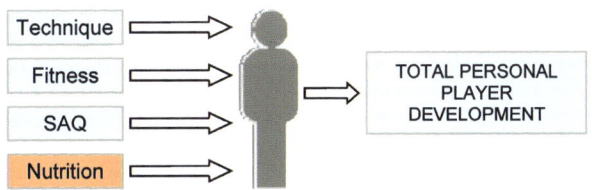

| Technique |
| Fitness |
| SAQ |
| Nutrition |

TOTAL PERSONAL PLAYER DEVELOPMENT

Remember: The following is only a guide and should be followed sensibly with any injuries or other problems. For certain exercises a dynamic warm-up is recommended (refer to page 8). Ask your coach if you are unsure of anything.

Ball Mastery and Control - A critical component of any players personal development.

Training Plan
Typical Football Season

If you follow the training codes at the correct times during both your on and off-season they will help you perform the activities and running intensities you face in a game easier. **GOOD LUCK!**

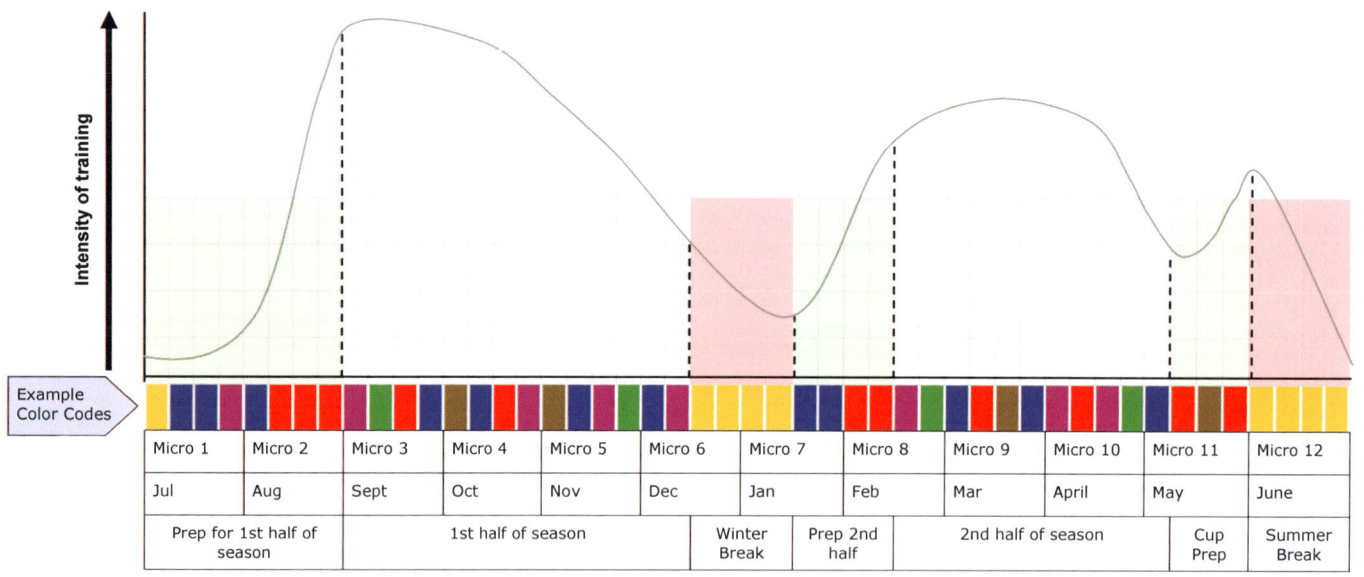

Micro 1	Micro 2	Micro 3	Micro 4	Micro 5	Micro 6	Micro 7	Micro 8	Micro 9	Micro 10	Micro 11	Micro 12
Jul	Aug	Sept	Oct	Nov	Dec	Jan	Feb	Mar	April	May	June
Prep for 1st half of season		1st half of season				Winter Break	Prep 2nd half	2nd half of season			Cup Prep	Summer Break

Using the Chart
The Training Plan above outlines what a typical competitive players season may look like. Use this chart as a high level reference as to the types of training codes you should be performing at various parts of the season and also off-season. This is only a 'typical season', yours may differ. Each week is assigned a color code for a particular training target. It will help you identify the type of training you should be doing for the appropriate phase of the season or off-season. The chart above has examples codes in it. Each color code has several training weeks which all have the same or similar training goals and are included to allow for more varied training.

Organized Training Plan
Plan out your season and note any potential breaks in your training routine (vacations, etc). Find a football pitch, ideally somewhere that takes you five minutes to jog to for the perfect warm-up and spend some time stretching. Some of the code activities can be done in a much smaller space, such as a back yard. Also, If possible try to find a training partner, it's great for motivation and you'll get much more out of the program.

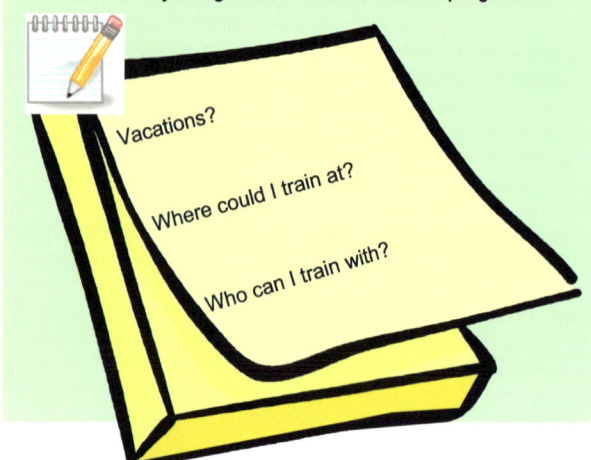

PTL Codes & Training Phases
Each color in on the chart above indicates a type of football specific training detailed in the codes (p9 - p24). This is a full year training program (including in season and off-season). The diagram above shows a suggested model and sequence of codes, but you are encouraged to make your own custom season program that fits your training goals and schedule.

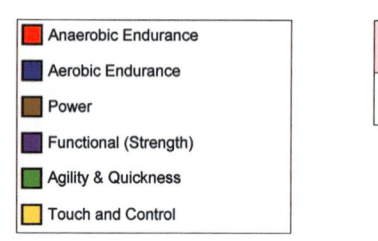

- Anaerobic Endurance
- Aerobic Endurance
- Power
- Functional (Strength)
- Agility & Quickness
- Touch and Control

- Team Training Breaks
- Preparation Phases

PTL and Your Season
Page 5 shows a typical football season for any competitive player. At various periods during the season the intensity and activity/practice type should be varied to allow players to peak at optimal times during the year. The PTL with its various codes is designed so that coaches and players can design their training schedules to peak at optimal points during the season.

Season Planner
On the next page is a blank season planner you can use to keep track of the codes you have to do each week. Use this like a calendar for your training. Write in the code names using a pen or pencil. Preferably pencil as sometimes coaches may change the codes they want to use during the season. And that's it!

Contents

What does it take to be the best?

Commitment
Determination
Passion
Dedication
Talent
Good players are made not born.

"The vision of a champion is someone who is bent over, drenched in sweat, at the point of exhaustion when no one else is watching."

- Anson Dorrance
US Womens National Team

"Instead of thinking 'I've had enough now', or 'I can't do it' or 'I can't hit it with my left foot', try to do more on your own and it will make you into a player."

- Frank Lampard
Chelsea FC and England National Team

"When you see a championship winning side, everyone has that fighter mentality, everyone wants to win. Everyone on the team has huge hearts. Its like they would die for you on the field. If you are having a bad game, or something's going wrong, you know they are going to be there to pick up the slack."

- Mia Hamm
US Womens National Team

"A champion is not someone who trains hard at practice……. Its someone who trains hard at practice and then goes home and does another 30 minutes."

- Darren Pitfield
PTL Author

"Champions do not become champions when they win the event, but in the hours, weeks, months and years they spend preparing for it. The victorious performance itself is merely the demonstration of their championship character.

- T. Alan Armstrong

"Players who are consistently the best at what they do, are those who are always trying to get better."

- Darren Pitfield
PTL Author

"Mentally, it makes you tougher and stronger knowing that you can run past or run more than any team you face."

- Carla Overbeck
US Womens National Team

"You get through practice 150%. You finish fitness faster than you did last time. You are training and working harder than you did yesterday, and you are going to work harder the next day than you did today."

- Brandi Chastain
US Womens National Team

"We are what we repeatedly do. Excellence is not an act, but a habit."

- Aristotle

"Everything is practice. Always strive to be the best, but never think you are the best."

- Pele
Santos FC, Brazil National Team

"I always wanted to be better than I was the day before."

- Mia Hamm
US Womens National Team

My Training Log
My Football Season

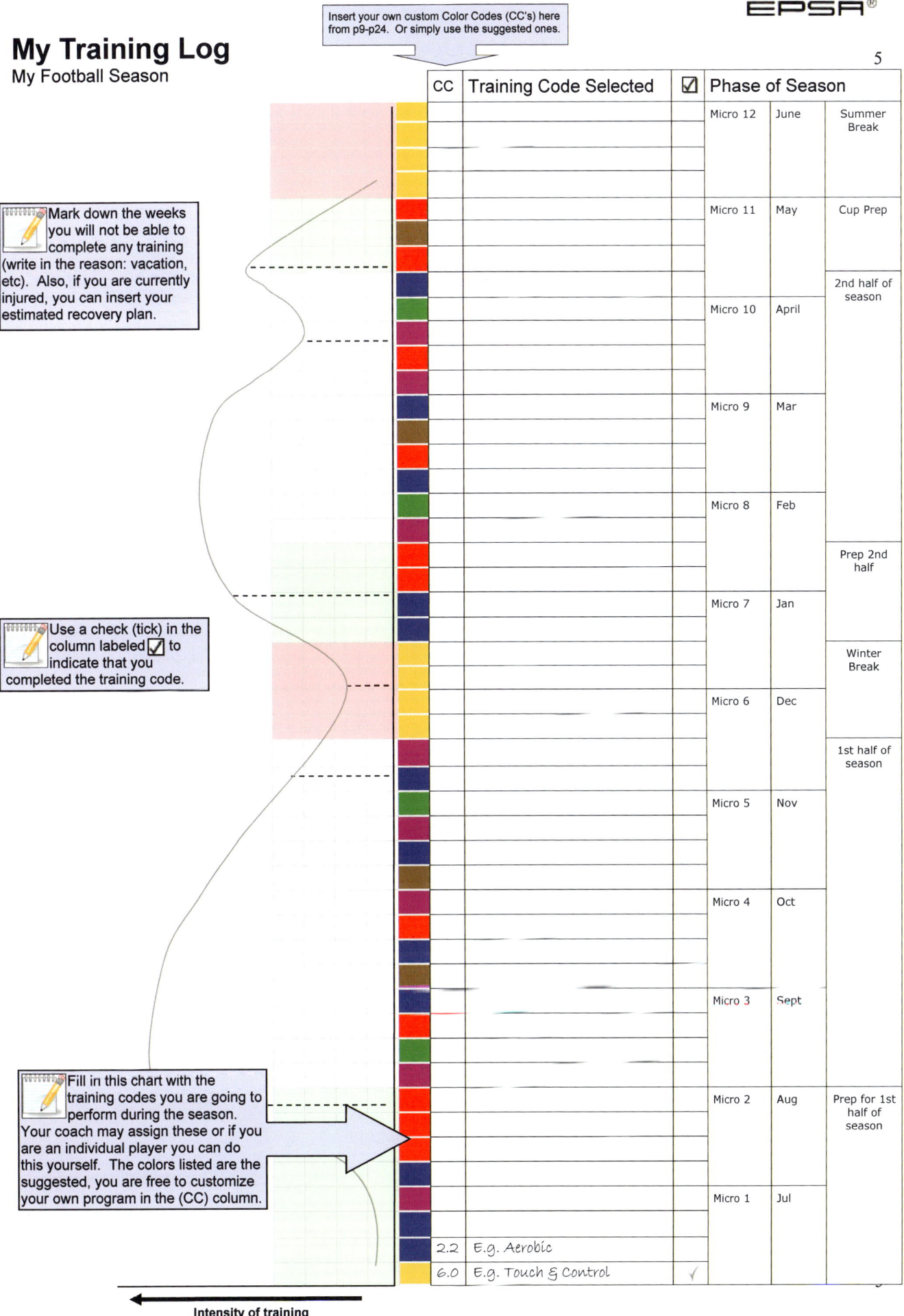

Insert your own custom Color Codes (CC's) here from p9-p24. Or simply use the suggested ones.

CC	Training Code Selected	☑	Phase of Season		
			Micro 12	June	Summer Break
			Micro 11	May	Cup Prep
					2nd half of season
			Micro 10	April	
			Micro 9	Mar	
			Micro 8	Feb	
					Prep 2nd half
			Micro 7	Jan	
					Winter Break
			Micro 6	Dec	
					1st half of season
			Micro 5	Nov	
			Micro 4	Oct	
			Micro 3	Sept	
			Micro 2	Aug	Prep for 1st half of season
			Micro 1	Jul	
2.2	E.g. Aerobic				
6.0	E.g. Touch & Control	✓			

Mark down the weeks you will not be able to complete any training (write in the reason: vacation, etc). Also, if you are currently injured, you can insert your estimated recovery plan.

Use a check (tick) in the column labeled ☑ to indicate that you completed the training code.

Fill in this chart with the training codes you are going to perform during the season. Your coach may assign these or if you are an individual player you can do this yourself. The colors listed are the suggested, you are free to customize your own program in the (CC) column.

← Intensity of training

Basic Soccer Fitness

Soccer is a 'multiple sprint sport', also known as 'intermittent' exercise, which means you perform many types of activities during a game at different intensities (shown in the charts below).

A game usually consists of periods of moderate 'aerobic' intensity activity (jogging, cruising) or rest (walking and standing), punctuated by brief periods of maximal sprinting ('an-aerobic' activity). Training should always be designed to mirror the nature and intensity of activities you do during a game.
Well structured fitness training will help you delay the onset of fatigue (burning in your muscles) and help you maintain your performance throughout the match or tournament.

> "REMEMBER SOCCER IS ABOUT SPRINTING, JOGGING, CRUISING, BACKWARD MOVEMENTS AND WALKING. BE GOOD AT THEM ALL. A SUPER FIT MARATHON RUNNER DOES NOT MAKE A GOOD SOCCER PLAYER!"

Components of Fitness in the PTL
The PTL is designed to train ALL aspects of fitness considered important to soccer. These include: Aerobic and Anaerobic endurance, speed, agility, acceleration, balance, co-ordination, muscular strength and endurance, power and quickness. Each of the codes are designed to train one of these areas.

Players spend 7 – 10% of total match time at the highest speed (sprinting). The intensities are in the ratio of 7:1 (aerobic vs anaerobic), which means slow vs. fast running.
When performing the activities in the PTL you will notice that there is a combination of all these activities so you can best develop a total fitness profile. Your seasons training is also structured in such a way to develop the foundations of fitness (aerobic fitness), before the others.

Action mode	Action rate of matches		Action rate of training		Total action rate, approx.
	A match	A season	A training	A season	Total season
	Match (n)	Season (n)	Training (n)	Season (n)	Total (n)
Passes	35	2100	100	22000	24000
Runs with ball	7	420	50	11000	11000
Headers	6	360	15	3300	3700
Shots	1	60	10	2200	2300
Tackles	7	420	15	3300	3700
Jumps	9	540	15	3300	3900
Turns	7	420	30	6600	7000

Table 2 Technical action rates in match and training conditions for a season.

Work-rate in a game and training
The activities of a top-class European (U-15B) player are shown in the charts. This gives you an idea of the kind of fitness demands we are looking at. He covered a total distance of 12.1 km (a long way!). His teammates averaged between 11.7 and 9.8 km. Players performed an average of 96 sprints ranging from 1.5 - 105 m. Average time for low intensity work was 51.6 sec and for high intensity work 3.7 sec.

It is important to perform these in the correct order or at the correct time of the year in order to maximize the benefits of the training and also avoid injury.

Summary of Activities During a Game:

- **2% with the ball**
- **11% sprinting**
- **20% cruising**
- **36% jogging**
- **7% backwards**
- **24% walking**

> Think about what types of activities you perform most in a game? How far do you think you run? Use post-it to answer.

> Think about what type of running your position requires? Think about where you play and how you move around the field? Make notes on the post-it note of what you've learnt!

Motion mode	Work rate of matches		Work rate of training		Total work rate	
	A match	A season	A training	A season	Total season	Steps, Approx.
	Dist. (km)	Dist. (km)	Dist. (km)	Dist. (km)	Dist. (km)	Number
Walking	3	180	2	440	620	890000
Jogging	5	300	4	880	1180	980000
Striding	1,5	90	3	660	750	420000
Sprinting	0,7	42	1,5	330	372	190000
Other	1	60	1,5	330	390	400000
Total	11,2	672	12	2640	3312	3000000
With ball	0,2	12	0,4	88	100	

Table 1 An evaluation of work rate in match and training conditions for a season.

EPSA®

Training Codes

TRAINING TYPE	No.	Code	Description	Pg.
Anaerobic	1.0	Red	Anaerobic I, High Intensity	9
	1.1	Red	Anaerobic II, High Intensity	10
	1.2	Red	Anaerobic III, Speed Endurance	11
Aerobic	2.0	Blue	Aerobic I, Low Intensity	12
	2.1	Blue	Aerobic II, Low Intensity	13
	2.2	Blue	Aerobic III, Low Intensity	14
	2.3	Blue	Aerobic IV, Low Intensity	15
	3.0	Brown	Power	16
Speed, Agility and Quickness	4.0	Green	SAQ I (Speed, Agility, Quickness)	17
	4.1	Green	SAQ II	18
	4.2	Green	SAQ III (Speed)	19
Functional	5.0	Purple	Functional I	20
	5.1	Purple	Functional II	21
Skill & Technique	6.0	Yellow	Touch & Receiving	22
	6.1	Yellow	Touch & Juggling	23
	6.2	Yellow	Touch & Dribbling	24

PTL Key

 = This symbol indicates that you should perform a warm-up before performing the training activity.

 = Cone or Marker

1.01 = Each Training activity also includes a specific numeric code (1.01, 2.04, etc) which a coach or trainer may reference.

Standard Pitch Size

Some of the activities in the PTL require the use of a full size football field. The standard dimensions of a full size field are shown on the right. Below are basic conversions if you need them.
12 Strides = 10yrds Approx.

10m = 10.93yrds
20m = 21.87yrds
50m = 54.68yrds

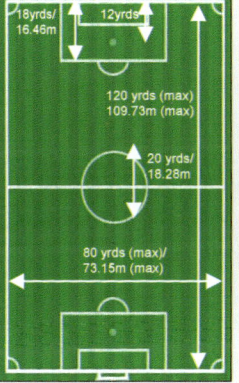

Heart Rate Calculations

In the PTL you will see references to 'HR' = Heart rate which allows us to monitor your work-rate to get the maximum benefits from an exercise. The manual refers to percentages of maximal heart rate (HR_{max}) for those who do not possess a heart rate monitor, the following 5 exercise intensity classifications should be used:

% HR_{max}	Type of Training	Perceived Exertion
Below 60%HR_{max}	Recovery	Very Easy
61 - 75%HR_{max}	Low Intensity	Easy to Comfortable
75 - 85%HR_{max}	Medium Intensity	Uncomfortable to Slightly Hard
86 - 93%HR_{max}	High Intensity	Hard to Very Hard
Over 93%HR_{max}	Maximal Effort	Maximal!!

Warm Up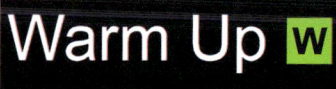

Dynamic Warm up for Soccer (3 Stages)

10 - 20 minutes – Duration is dependent on the age of the athlete and their current physical condition (older = longer). The following is an example of a dynamic soccer warm up which mimic the actions used in training and competition that is designed to:

+ Raise the body temperature

+ Increase muscle elasticity and neuromuscular function

+ Increases heart rate, respiratory rate and blood flow

+ Prepare mentally for a game

It is performed in three stages starting with general exercises and ending with soccer specific activities. Keep athletes moving and gradually increase the intensity of the activities.

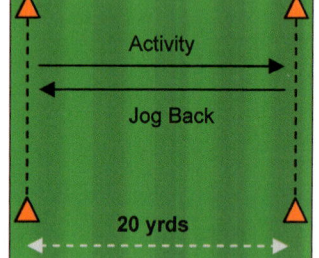

Step 1- Aerobic activity: Perform a five minute, low-level aerobic activity, such as jogging, or technical work with the ball, passing/driving balls to partner(s) (**5 MINS**)

Step 2 - Dynamic Flexibility: These exercises incorporate active movements to stretch the hips and pelvic region targeting hamstrings, hip flexors, gluteus and groin, which are important for injury prevention in soccer. (**7 MINS**)

Alternate Toe Touches: With legs wide apart, alternate touching hand to the outside of the opposite little toe.

Heel to Rear: Pull heel to rear and hold for a three count

Knee to Chest: Standing pull one knee to chest and hold for a three count

Forward Leg Swings/Back Leg Swings

Lateral Leg Swings

Hands on hips: thrust pelvic out and rotate in a large circle (hula hoop style)

Hand Walks: Starting in a push up position, walk feet up to hands, then walk hands out to a push up position and repeat, keeping back flat.

Step 3 - Movement Preparation: Exercises that imitate specific activities performed over a 20-yard distance. (**10 MINS**) Perform each of the actives for 20 yrds, then walk that 20 yards back to the start. Then perform the next activity and so on until they are all complete. Stop after this step for individual training or training log activity preparation. See Fig. 1.

1. Back Pedals	8. Butt Kickers
2. Skip Forward/Backwards	9. High knee walk/skips
3. Jog Forward and circle arms forward	10. High Knees
4. Lateral shuffles,	11. Lunge Walks
5. Carrioca	12. Defensive back shuffles
6. Inside/Outs Skip sideway lift back	13. Leg raise + twist to other side
7. Toe Walks	14. Accelerations

Activity

Jog Back

20 yrds

Step 4 - Game Preparation: If you are preparing for a game your team coach will perform drills and exercises for Step 4. These will be designed to best help the team, and may include possession drills or various functional practices, set pieces, etc.

"Sign the columns below when you have completed that days training. Start with the column furthest to the left. For youth players have your parents sign/initial in the column also to verify that your coach/manager can monitor your progress.

Personal Fitness Routine 1.0
🟥 CODE RED

Anaerobic I

**Parent/Guardian Signature
AND Player Signature**

MONDAY If No Team Training Perform the following 1.01	**5 stage shuttles** W Set up as in the diagram. Markers (cones) are placed 5-7 yards apart, up to 25 yards out. Sprint (100%) in pattern shown Rest for 2 mins and then repeat Perform 7-10 reps. Also replace the grey back tracking runs with back peddles (i.e. sprint out 10yrds, back peddle 5yrds)					
TUESDAY If No Team Training Perform the following 1.02	**Fartlek Runs** W Set up markers as shown in the diagram: 1-2 = 5yrd, 3-4 = 15yrds 2-3 = 10yrds, 4-5 = 20yrds, 5-6 = 25ryds. Start at 1, sprint to 2 (100%). Rest for 5s. Sprint to 3 (100%). Rest for 4 secs. Continue using the times shown. Rest for 3 mins. Repeat 5 to 10 times.					
WEDNESDAY If No Team Training Perform the following 1.03	**1/2 Field Shuttles** W (Find a soccer field) Sprint up to the 6 yard line and back Rest at goal line, for 10-15 seconds. Sprint again to the 18 yrd line (b) and back. After a second brake of 10-15 seconds, sprint to midfield and back and rest 10-15 secs. Then perform the same for (d) and (e). Rest for 2 min, repeat 4 times. Decrease the rest periods to 5 seconds to increase the intensity of the exercise.					
THURSDAY If No Team Training Perform the following 1.04	**Tick Tocks** W Sprint to a marker and walk back, and across to next, no rest (Use the walk back as the rest period). Use any items for markers: A = 20yrds B = 30yrds C = 40yrds D = 50yrds 100% **every sprint.** Rest for 2 min between bouts Repeat 4 times					
FRIDAY	**REST**					
SATURDAY	**GAME** OR **REST**					
SUNDAY	**GAME** OR **REST**					

"Training focusing on **anaerobic endurance** (high intensity running and sprinting). This is a hard training week. Good training for all players, but particularly good for mid-fielders, wide-players, forwards. It is vital that soccer players are quick and are able to **perform repeated sprints throughout the whole match**.

Be sure to **sprint maximally (100%)** on the sprint phases of the exercises. Just as important is to take the correct amount of rest time!"

Personal Fitness Routine 1.1

 **CODE RED**

Anaerobic II

Parent/Guardian Signature
AND Player Signature

MONDAY	**Multi-Sprint** W				
If No Team Training Perform the following	Mark off distances by walking or measuring (10yrds = 12 strides). Perform the following: 8x20yrds (30s sprint & rest for 20's) 6x40yrds (45s sprint & rest for 40's) 4x60yrds (60s sprint & rest for 50's) 2x80yrds (75s sprint & rest for 80's) 1x100yrds (90s sprint & rest for 100's) Maximal sprints and walk back.				
1.11					
TUESDAY	**Jingle Jangles** W				
If No Team Training Perform the following	Set up 2 markers 10yrds apart. You will need a ball at the start line. Sprint up and back 20 times (200yrd total). Complete in under 50secs -1 min. Rest for 1 minute between sets by juggling a ball. Perform 8 sets. Every 3rd go rest an extra 15 secs.				
1.12					
WEDNESDAY	**Super Sets** W				
If No Team Training Perform the following	Mark out 120yrds and 40yrds. Sprint 120yrds in 18secs (20 secs < U-14). Jog back (120yrds) to start line in 30secs (35 secs < U-14). Rest for 25 secs on the line. Then sprint 40yrd shuttles (up and back to 40yrd marker three times). No more than 50 secs. Rest for 1.15 mins (1.45 for < U-14). Perform 3-5 sets.				
1.13					
THURSDAY	**Box Of Death** W				
If No Team Training Perform the following	Layout 8 cones in the pattern shown . Each Cone (Marker) is 20 yrs apart. Start by sprinting from cone 1 to cone 2 and jog the rest back to 1 again. Then sprint from 1 to 3 and jog the rest. Then 1-4, etc...Until sprint all the way around. 4 min Rest & Repeat.				
1.14					
FRIDAY	**REST**				
SATURDAY	**GAME** OR **REST**				
SUNDAY	**GAME** OR **REST**				

"Training focusing on **anaerobic endurance** (high intensity running and sprinting). This is a hard training week. Good training for all players, but particularly good for mid-fielders, wide-players, forwards. It is vital that soccer players are quick and are able to **perform repeated sprints throughout the whole match**.

Be sure to **sprint maximally (100%)** on the sprint phases of the exercises. Just as important is to take the correct amount of rest time!"

Personal Skill Routine 1.2

 **CODE RED**

Anaerobic III (Speed Endurance)

Parent/Guardian Signature
AND Player Signature

MONDAY

If No Team Training Perform the following

Speed Endurance W

Start by walking across to the left hand bottom corner of the field from the right corner. Then follow the pattern shown from the Start position.

Perform the following exercise as close to the appropriate intensities as shown below. Each lap should take approximately ± 4 mins. Perform 3 laps. Therefore 1 Set = ± 12 mins.

Take a 5 min passive recovery between each set. Perform another Set of 3 Laps (±12 mins). Total exercise duration approx. = ± 29 mins.

⋯⋯▶ Walking

- - -▶ Jogging

— —▶ Cruising (80%)

——▶ Sprinting (Maximal)

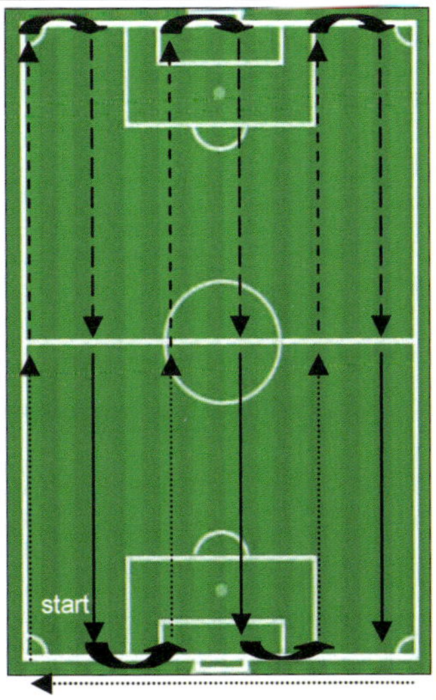

1.21

TUESDAY — **REST**

WEDNESDAY

If No Team Training Perform the following

Speed Endurance—Loop Run W

Mark out 4 cones on a regulation size field as shown below. You will need clearly marked 18yrd boxes for this activity.

Perform 10 loop runs (These should take ± 15 secs on each side of the main diagonal loop. Each loop run is followed by 45 secs of recovery (i.e. walking) around the cone on the edge of the 6 yard area. The duration of this recovery period can be altered to fit your fitness level.

One set should take you approx. 10 mins.

Rest for 4 mins between sets.

Perform 2 sets in total.

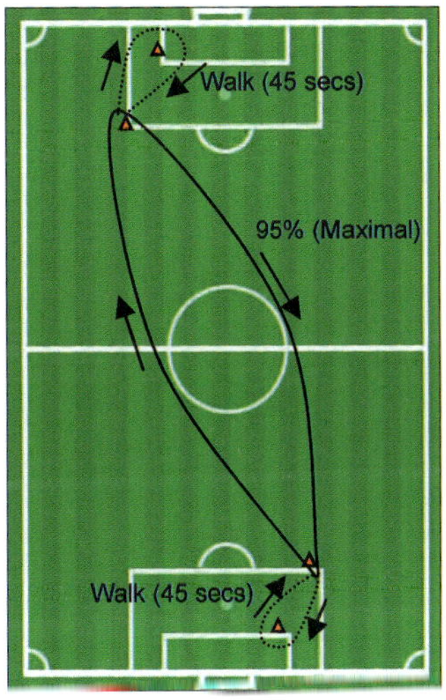

Walk (45 secs)

95% (Maximal)

Walk (45 secs)

1.22

THURSDAY

If No Team Training Perform the following

Light Aerobic

30 cycling between 60 - 70% HRmax
OR
30 min running between 75 - 85% HRmax (do not exceed this range)

1.23

FRIDAY — **REST**

SATURDAY — **GAME** OR **REST**

SUNDAY — **GAME** OR **REST**

"Speed Endurance gives you the ability to run at top speeds for extended periods of time. This type of training helps your body to clear lactate and reduce the formation of lactate in your muscles. Which means you will be able to sustain your sprints for longer in games."

Personal Fitness Routine 2.0
■ CODE BLUE

Aerobic I

Parent/Guardian Signature
AND Player Signature

MONDAY If No Team Training Perform the following ⟩ 2.01	**3 Mile Jog** Aerobic Endurance 3 mile run (preferably on grass and **with a ball**). Heart rate should be between 120 – 160 b/min. If <120 b/min you are not working hard enough, if >160 b/min slow down.	Note: 4 1/2 laps of an average full size soccer field = 1 mile. 3 miles = 9 1/2 laps of field.				
TUESDAY If No Team Training Perform the following ⟩ 2.02	**Aerobic soccer Runs 1** Ⓦ Find a marked soccer field. Run all the way down one half on the side-line back diagonally to the other side of the half way line. Then jog easy back across to the start. Repeat 3 circuits. Rest for 3 mins then repeat. Do 4 sets.	*(field diagram: Start, 90% Run, Jog)*				
WEDNESDAY If No Team Training Perform the following ⟩ 2.03	**Aerobic soccer Runs 2** Ⓦ (Find a marked soccer field. This is a straight forward interval drill that doesn't require any formal setup. Simply run laps around the field, alternating between light jogging and sprints. You're supposed to change pace any time you reach a corner flag or the midfield line. Perform 5-10 laps continuous.	*(field diagram: Sprint, Jog)*				
THURSDAY	**REST**					
FRIDAY If No Team Training Perform the following ⟩ 2.04	**Bangsbo Intermittent** Ⓦ Use items or objects to mark out the course. Approx. 20yrds between the orange cones. 10yrds between yellow. Start with 5 min continuous circuits. As fitness improves increase to (10-20 mins).	*(diagram: Side steps, backpeddle, cruise, jog, Sprint Zig-zags, Sprint, walk, jog)*				
SATURDAY	**GAME** OR **REST**					
SUNDAY	**GAME** OR **REST**					

"Training focus for this week is on **aerobic endurance** (low intensity running and working on your wind during a game). All soccer players need to cover long distances during games. This training week will help you to **run for longer periods in games** and also recover from games faster.

Be sure to **train at the intensities** stated in the exercise descriptions. All players need a good aerobic base to be a high level soccer player."

13

Personal Fitness Routine 2.1
■ CODE BLUE

Aerobic II

Parent/Guardian Signature
AND Player Signature

MONDAY *If No Team Training Perform the following* 2.11	**Aerobic soccer Runs 1** Use items or cone to set up 20x30yrd Grid. Start at the bottom left cone. Play ball to next cone, Follow (sprint) and stop before reaches next cone. Dribble ball to next where ball is left until picked up next time around. Repeat from other side, continue for 5 mins. Perform 3 reps, rest 3mins between.					
TUESDAY *If No Team Training Perform the following* 2.12	**Intervals 1** W Set up the course shown to the right. Run at 75-85% of max sprint speed along the long sides (40yrds) and then walk/jog the short sides 15-20yrds. Must complete the short side walks/jogs in 12secs before sprinting again.					
WEDNESDAY *If No Team Training Perform the following* 2.13	**Fartlek Runs II** Can be performed around a soccer field or straight distance. Split a continuous run into these sections: Where run = 80% max Rest = slow jog Full Rest = Stopped	**Intensity Pattern:** 15s run, 15s rest, 30s run, 30s rest, 45s run, 45s rest, 60s run, 60s rest, 90s run, 90s rest, + FULL REST for 2 mins. Repeat this 3 times.				
THURSDAY *If No Team Training Perform the following* 2.14	**Pyramid Runs** Perform the following running pattern: Run 1min , jog 30s, Run 2 min, jog 30s, Run 3 min, jog 30s, Run 4 min, jog 30s, Run 3 min, jog 30s, Run 2 min, jog 30s, Run 1 min, rest. Runs should be at 76% max effort. Jogging should be a slow jog.					
FRIDAY	**REST**					
SATURDAY	**GAME** OR **REST**					
SUNDAY	**GAME** OR **REST**					

"Training focusing for this week is on **aerobic endurance** (low intensity running and working on your wind during a game). All soccer players need to cover long distances during game. This training week will help you to **run for longer in games** and also recover from games faster.

Be sure to **train at the intensities** stated in the exercise descriptions. All players need a good aerobic base to be a high level soccer player."

Personal Skill Routine 2.2
■ CODE BLUE

Aerobic III

MONDAY If No Team Training Perform the following 2.21	**Intermittent Running and Speed Work** W From the start, accelerate 10m. Then undertake an active recovery loop (jogging) to the edge of the field and back. After this loop, walk to the red cone. From the red cone, accelerate 20m, then perform another active recovery loop to the edge of the field and back. After this loop, walk to the blue cone and from here, accelerate 30m. Active recovery loop to the edge of the field. Now walk to the white cone from here, accelerate 40m and perform the active recovery to complete 1 Set. 2.5 min to complete Set and recover walk back to start. Perform a 2nd Set 2.5 min to complete Set and recover walk back to start. Perform a 3rd Set (300m of intermittent acceleration running in total).	(field diagram: 40m, 30m, 20m, 10m, walk, start)				
TUESDAY	**REST**					
WEDNESDAY If No Team Training Perform the following 2.22	**Intermittent Running 2** W From the start (bottom left corner of a regulation size field), perform the appropriate intensities shown. Each Lap has a small variation: On Lap 1 run around cone 1, and so on up to cone 4 on Lap 4. The 'cruise' running should be ¾ pace (the HR that it will elicit should be approx. ~ 93%HR_{max}). 4 Laps equals = 1 Set (± 8 mins). Take a 3 min recovery break. Perform another Set, This time running around cone 4 on the first Lap and working down to cone 1 on the 4th Lap (± 8 mins). Take a 3 min recovery break. Perform a 3rd Set, this time running around cone 1 on the first Lap and working down to cone 4 on the 4th Lap (± 8 min).	(field diagram: walk, 3/4cruise, 3/4cruise, jog, jog, cones 4 3 2 1, start, 3/4cruis, 3/4cruis)				
THURSDAY If No Team Training Perform the following 2.23	**Light Aerobic** 30 cycling between 60 - 70% HR_{max} **OR** 30 min running between 75 - 85% HR_{max} (do not exceed this range)					
FRIDAY	**REST**					
SATURDAY	**GAME** OR					
SUNDAY	**GAME** OR **REST**					

"This is another aerobic week in which we are aiming to improve the efficiency of our muscles to use oxygen to produce energy, as opposed to the limited glucose stored in our muscles. Improving the way your body uptake oxygen will help you run for longer periods at lower intensities and save your explosive energy supplies in your muscles for those high intensity sprints you will be making."

Personal Skill Routine 2.3
■ CODE BLUE

Aerobic IV

Parent/Guardian Signature
AND Player Signature

MONDAY If No Team Training Perform the following 2.31	**Intermittent Loop Running** W Follow the circuit from the 'Start' around the cones at the desired intensities. The sequence of activities from the start is: ¾ pace run, jog, sprint, walk , ¾ pace run, jog, sprint, jog, ¾ pace run and a final recovery walk. Attempt to maintain the intensities displayed and not blend jogs into cruises, etc. Perform slow deceleration after the sprints in order to avoid injury. Perform 4 laps going on every 2.5 mins. Set 1 Duration = ± 10 min. 3 min recovery break. Perform a second Set, this time starting from the opposite corner. This allows you to work on turns in the other direction. Set 2 Duration = ± 10 min.	*(field diagram: 3/4 cruise, jog, walk, sprint, sprint, jog, jog, 3/4 cruise, 3/4 cruise, Start, walk)*				
TUESDAY	**REST**					
WEDNESDAY If No Team Training Perform the following 2.32	**Intermittent Running - Pitch Figure 8** Perform a figure of 8 running pattern around a regulation size field by follow the arrows from the 'Start' (bottom left). The running should be a cruise (¾ pace) (Approx. 86%HR_{max}, peak 96%HR_{max}). Attempt to be consistent in lap times (±5 secs) and maintain a consistent running speed throughout each lap. Modify your speed if needed if your lap times are progressively decreasing or increasing. They should be consistent. Practice good agility when changing directions to complete the lap. Corners should be taken fairly tight, it may be necessary to slow slightly before each corner. Perform 5 Laps of the above exercise (± 1.30 min per lap). Take a 40 secs recovery break in-between laps. Set 1 Duration = ± 10 mins 3 min recovery break. Repeat for a 2nd Set with 50 secs recovery breaks in-between laps. Set 2 Duration = ± 10 mins	*(field diagram: 3/4 cruise, Start)*				
THURSDAY If No Team Training Perform the following 2.33	**Light Aerobic** 30 cycling between 60 - 70% HRmax **OR** 30 min running between 75 - 85% HRmax (do not exceed this range)					
FRIDAY	**REST**					
SATURDAY	**GAME** OR					
SUNDAY	**GAME** OR **REST**					

"This is another variation of an aerobic training week. It has a mixture of intermittent work designed to mirror the activities that you do in a game. This is helping us to build a solid aerobic fitness base from which all the other fitness work we do is based."

Personal Fitness Routine 3.0
■ CODE BROWN

Power

MONDAY If No Team Training Perform the following 3.01	**Hill Climbs** W Aerobic Endurance as warm-up. Run approx 1 mile run (to a hill or incline) Heart rate should be between 120 – 170 b/min. if <120 you are not working hard enough, if >170 slow down. Practice the activities 1/2 way up (25yrds) the slope and sprint the remaining 1/2 (powering up maximally). Use arms and thighs to drive (accelerate) up the second 25 yrs. Walk down to recover and rest another 20 sec's. Repeat as many times until failure (total FATIGUE).	1. Walking Lunges (x2) 2. 2 Footed Bounds (x2) 3. Straight Leg Jumps (x2) 4. Back-Peddle (x2) 5. High Knees (x2) 6. Butt Kickers (x2)				
TUESDAY If No Team Training Perform the following 3.02	**Power Circuit 1** W Use items or cone to set up 20x30yrd Grid. Start at bottom left cone (work around). Lap One = Hop right leg Lap Two = Hop left leg (Bend Knee on landing) Perform 2 laps and then rest for 3 mins, juggle for 2 mins, Then repeat for another 2 mins.					
WEDNESDAY If No Team Training Perform the following 3.03	**Plyometric 1** W Perform the following activities over 15yrds then walk back to recover: Repeat each activity and walk (x6). 1) Walking Lunges holding ball above your head. 2) 2 Footed Bounds (Bend knees on landing, pause in between.)					
THURSDAY If No Team Training Perform the following 3.04	**Semi Circle Power/Agility** W Each cone is 5 yrds apart as shown. Start at the middle cone, sprint to 1, back-peddle back to 0. Repeat to cone 2, back-peddle, Repeat all the way round. Rest 2 mins. Repeat Doing defensive jockeys instead of b-peddles.					
FRIDAY	**REST**					
SATURDAY	**GAME** OR **REST**					
SUNDAY	**GAME** OR **REST**					

"Training focusing for this week is on **aerobic endurance** (low intensity running and working on your wind during a game). All soccer players need to cover long distances during game. This training week will help you to **run for longer in games** and also recover from games faster.

Be sure to **train at the intensities** stated in the exercise descriptions. All players need a good aerobic base to be a high level soccer player."

Personal Fitness Routine 4.0

🟩 **CODE GREEN**

Agility and Quickness I

MONDAY	**50 Yrd "Ajax" Shuttle** 🅆 Mark two lines 10 yards apart. The player begins at line A, then runs and touches line B, plants and returns to A. Repeat 5 times. Scores under 10 sec's are considered good. A deficiency indicates lack of functional leg strength. Repeat 7 times with 1 m in rests in between. Test your sprint endurance, try and maintain low times. Time yourself.					
If No Team Training Perform the following						
4.01						
TUESDAY	**Illinois Agility Test** 🅆 Sprint and weave around the cones as indicated. This activity tests change of direction, body awareness, body control and footwork. Any time under 15 sec's is considered good. Repeat 7 times. Record your best times and try and beat them. Perform this with a ball also.					
If No Team Training Perform the following						
4.02						
WEDNESDAY	**T Test Agility** 🅆 Set out markers as shown. Maximal intensity (100%). Sprint to the centre cone, Shuffle to A, back to B, shuffle back to the centre cone and backpeddle to the start/finish. 2 mins rest between reps. 4-6 reps. Perform with no shuffling also.					
If No Team Training Perform the following						
4.03						
THURSDAY	**Super Shuttle** 🅆 Set a series of cones out as shown. Follow the instructions in the diagram from start to finish. Push yourself in all directions with short strides and good acceleration. Time yourself also.					
If No Team Training Perform the following						
4.04						
FRIDAY	**REST**					
SATURDAY	**GAME** OR **REST**					
SUNDAY	**GAME** OR **REST**					

"Training focusing for this week is on **agility** (the ability to turn and twist, change direction during a game). Agility is a hugely underestimated aspect of a soccer players conditioning. Think about how many times in a game you change direction quickly, accelerate, decelerate, move laterally, jump for headers, back peddle, etc."

Personal Skill Routine 4.1
▣ CODE GREEN

Agility and Quickness II

**Parent/Guardian Signature
AND Player Signature**

MONDAY If No Team Training Perform the following 4.11	**Agility - 18 Yrd Box** Ⓦ Perform 3 Laps of the circuit shown. Go on every 2 min (1 Set = 6 min). (2 mins includes the activity and rest). Attempt to perform with sharp cuts and turns, maintaining good balance. 3 min recovery after set 1. Perform a 2nd Set, continuing to go on every 2 mins. Total Activity duration = ± 15 mins. Approx. 300yrds of mixed activities.	(jog / accelerate / backp. / walk diagram)				
TUESDAY If No Team Training Perform the following 4.12	**Fast Feet Work** Perform fast feet activities (See Fast Feet Exercises below), then sprint 10yrds, decelerate, before turning and accelerating 10yrds back to start. Repeat x4. Perform each sprint maximally. Your work/rest recovery ratio should be 1 – 10 so as not to create fatigue during agility drills. HR should be back to 60 – 65% HR_{max} prior to each rep. Attempt to explode out of the fast feet cones with a low centre of gravity and high stride frequency .	Fast Feet Exercises / sprint / 10yrds diagram <u>Fast Feet Exercises (Variations):</u> 1) One foot in each space – accelerating through 2) Side shuffles – technique then speed 3) Lateral steps – leading with left leg 4) Lateral steps – leading with right leg				
WEDNESDAY	**REST**					
THURSDAY If No Team Training Perform the following 4.13	**Reverse 'L' Run** Ⓦ Perform this agility circuit by starting at point A: Sprint forwards to B, Backpedal back to A, Side step left to C, Side step right (facing opposite direction) to D, sprint forwards to E (1 Rep = ± 15 secs). Perform 6 reps of the circuit, with maximal effort, rest for 90 seconds between reps. Record your times and attempt to better those times as you progress.	(Reverse L Run diagram with points A, B, C, D, E, 10m markings, sprint + b.paddle, side-step, accelerate)				
FRIDAY	**REST**					
SATURDAY	**GAME** OR					
SUNDAY	**GAME** OR **REST**					

"Training focus for this week is on **agility** (the ability to turn and twist, change direction during a game). Agility is a hugely underestimated aspect of a soccer players conditioning. Think about how many times in a game you change direction quickly, accelerate, decelerate, move laterally, jump for headers, back peddle, etc."

Personal Skill Routine 4.2
▮ CODE GREEN
Agility & Quickness III

Parent/Guardian Signature
AND Player Signature

MONDAY *If No Team Training Perform the following*	### Acceleration/Speed Training ▮ Set out cones as shown in the diagram to the right and perform the following pattern of sprints. 6x 10yrds — Recovery 20sec in between each sprint. Then rest 1min. 4x 20yrds — Recovery 40sec in between each sprint. Then rest 1min. 2x 30yrds — Recovery 80sec in between each sprint. Then rest 1min. 4x 20yrds — Recovery 40sec in between each sprint. Then rest 1min. 6x 10yrds — Recovery 20sec in between each sprint. Perform each sprint maximally taking the full breaks. With a high work/rest ratio (1:15) you should avoid fatigue. Ensure that your HR is back to Approx. 60 – 65% HR_{max} prior to each rep. A very slow walk back to the start is a good way of determining your recovery time between sprints. Total sprint distance of 280yrds. Total exercise duration = 15 minutes. 4.21	[diagram: 30yrds, 20yrds, 10yrds, start]		
TUESDAY *If No Team Training Perform the following*	### Speed Training ▮ Set out cones as shown in the diagram to the right. Approx. 60x40yrd area. Perform a circuit of 4 sprints starting at the top right hand corner. Perform each sprint maximally. Rest for 2 minutes after each circuit. On lap 2 repeat the circuit in reverse order, (i.e., 60yrd sprint first, 20yrd sprint last). Rest for 2 mins again. Repeat the circuit the original way again until you have completed 4 circuits. Total sprint distance = 600yrds. 4.22	[diagram: Start, 20yrds sprint, 40yrds walk, 30yrds walk, 30yrds sprint, 40yrds sprint, 20yrds walk, Finish, 60yrds sprint]		
WEDNESDAY	**REST**			
THURSDAY *If No Team Training Perform the following*	### Acceleration/Deceleration ▮ Set out cones as shown in the diagram to the right. Perform the running intensities shown in the diagram, then perform a Recovery Walk back to the Start. Repeat x 6. Rest for 2 minutes. If your HR is above 80% and you are experiencing fatigue you will need to increase your recovery duration. **OR** Perform 15 squats then rest for 45 secs. Repeat x3 = 1 Set. Rest for 2 mins and repeat. Take a 2 min break. Then jump rope (basic) for 4 mins. Rest 1 min and repeat for a second 4 mins. 4.23	[diagram: start ... finish; jog sprint jog sprint jog sprint; 10y 10y 20y 20y 30y 30y]		
FRIDAY	**REST**			
SATURDAY	**GAME** OR **REST**			
SUNDAY	**GAME** OR **REST**			

"In this week we are aiming to improve speed power and quickness of the mark. We are working to improve the efficiency of your muscle fibers and also increase the number of anaerobic muscle fibers. This training week will help you accelerate and decelerate quicker in a game."

Personal Fitness Routine 5.0
■ CODE Purple
Functional I

Parent/Guardian Signature AND Player Signature

MONDAY								
If No Team Training Perform the following	1. This circuit consists of 3 cycles. Work down the list of exercises in cycle 1, then cycle 2 and finally cycle 3 to complete the circuit. Take 30 sec breaks in-between exercises if needed. 2. Each cycle gets progressively harder (i.e. the number of repetitions for each exercise increases).							

Press-Up Squat Circuit 🟩 W   **Number of Cycle**

	1	**2**	**3**

Regular Push-up

10   12   15

Standing Double Leg Squat

10   15   20

Abdominal Crunches

20   25   30

5.01

TUESDAY	TRAINING or REST

WEDNESDAY

If No Team Training Perform the following

Standing Single Leg Squat

10   12   15

Raised Abdominal Crunches

20   25   30

Front Raised Press Up

10   15   20

Oblique Crunches

20   25   30

5.02

THURSDAY	TRAINING or REST
FRIDAY	TRAINING or REST
SATURDAY	GAME OR REST
SUNDAY	GAME OR REST

"By doing regular bodyweight circuits you will improve the strength and endurance of the specific muscles that you need for football. In Week One of these activity types you want to take it quite easy. These circuits kill two birds with one stone. As well as working on your fitness, your heart and lungs, at the same time they strengthen the muscles that you specifically use for football."

Personal Fitness Routine 5.1
■ CODE Purple

Functional II

Parent/Guardian Signature
AND Player Signature

MONDAY

If No Team Training Perform the following

1. This circuit consists of 3 cycles. Work down the list of exercises in cycle 1, then cycle 2 and finally cycle 3 to complete the circuit. Take 30 sec breaks in-between exercises if needed.
2. Each cycle gets progressively harder (i.e. the number of repetitions for each exercise increases).

Press-Up Lunge Circuit [W]

Exercise	Cycle Number 1	2	3
Regular Push-Up	10	12	15
Forward Lunges	10	12	15
Abdominal Crunches	20	25	30
Close Arm Press Up	8	10	12

5.11

TUESDAY — TRAINING or REST

WEDNESDAY

If No Team Training Perform the following

Exercise	Cycle Number 1	2	3
Side Lunges	10	12	15
Raised Abdominal Crunches	20	25	30
Staggered Arm Press Up	10	12	15
Multi-directional Lunges	10	12	15

5.12

THURSDAY — TRAINING or REST

FRIDAY — TRAINING or REST

SATURDAY — GAME OR REST

SUNDAY — GAME OR REST

"By doing regular bodyweight circuits you will improve the strength and endurance of the specific muscles that you need for football. In Week One of these activity types you want to take it quite easy. These circuits kill two birds with one stone. As well as working on your fitness, your heart and lungs, at the same time they strengthen the muscles that you specifically use for football."

Personal Skill Routine 6.0
☐ CODE YELLOW

Touch & Control

**Parent/Guardian Signature
AND Player Signature**

MONDAY *If No Team Training Perform the following* 6.01	**Dribbling/Close control Practice** Set up 7 markers/cones. 2 steps apart from each other in a line. Dribble around all the cones and back (with a ball) Time yourself, 25 – 30 secs is Good, < 20 – 25 secs is Excellent, < 20 is Outstanding Try with both feet. Try with your weaker foot!. Place the markers closer together (1 stride apart). Try with a smaller ball, size 2 or 3, tennis ball.					
TUESDAY *If No Team Training Perform the following* 6.02	**Figure 8's** 2 cones are 3yrds apart. Dribble around in a figure of 8 shape. 1. Right Foot Only (1min) 2. Left Foot Only (1min) 3. Instep Only (1 min) 4. Out-step Only (1min) Repeat the above 4 times. Rest 30s between.					
WEDNESDAY *If No Team Training Perform the following* 6.03	**Skills Training 1** Practice your turns, 180 degrees. Practice your Stop/Starts (25 reps of each) (25 reps of each) 1. Cruyff Turn 1. Step On (Double Step on Also) 2. Drag Back (Pull Back) 2. Pull Push 3. Inside Hook 3. Step Kick 4. Outside Hook 4. Waves (High & Slow Waves) 5. Slap Turn 5. Shimmy (Fake to cut inside)					
THURSDAY *If No Team Training Perform the following* 6.04	**Skills Training 2** Practice your feints (Moves to go past a defender, 1v1) (25 reps of each) 1. Side Step (Stanley Matthews) (Single and Double) 2. Step Over 3. Scissors (Single and Double) 4. Rivalino/Careca 5. Fake Shot					
FRIDAY *If No Team Training Perform the following* 6.05	**Wall Work** Find a wall you can kick a ball against. Start 10 yrds away from the wall with the following sequences: 1. 20 Right Ft Sidefoots + 20 Left Sidefoots (2 Touch, Control then Pass) 10yrds 2. 20 Right Ft Sidefoots + 20 Right Sidefoots (1 Touch) 10yrds to 1 yrd. Move in towards the wall with each pass so reaction time becomes less. 3. Chip the ball in the air against the wall and control. Repeat 20 times. 15yrds 4. Shoot at the wall with your laces (driven shots) 20 Left & 20 Right Foot. 20yrds Focus on technique before power on all the above!					
SATURDAY	**GAME** OR **REST**					
SUNDAY	**GAME** OR **REST**					

"Training focus for this week is on '**Ball Mastery** and **Touch**' (the ability to control, turn, receive, beat an opponent 1vs1). Players should be comfortable with performing these ball mastery moves to the point they are automatic. If you don't know how to do the moves please ask your coach for directions."

Personal Skill Routine 6.1
☐ CODE YELLOW
Juggling & Touch

**Parent/Guardian Signature
AND Player Signature**

MONDAY If No Team Training Perform the following 6.11	**Beginners U-11 to U-12** 1. Feet 50 Times. Juggle the ball with your feet 50 times in a row. Feet Only. 2. Thighs 25 Times. Juggle the ball with your thighs 25 times in a row. Max of 5 consecutive touches on one thigh. 3. Head 10 Times. Juggle the ball with your head 10 times in a row. 4. 2 Left and 2 Right with Feet x6. Juggle the ball with your left foot 2 times in a row then your right foot 2 times in a row. Continue until you reach 6 times without dropping ball or 24 touches. 5. 2 Head, 2 Shoulder Juggle (shoulder back up to your head), 2 more Head, and catch. 6. ½ Around-the-World x5. Sequence = Right foot, right thigh, left thigh, left foot. Continue around 5 times. 7. Reverse the direction of ½ Around-the-World (Start on your left foot). **Advanced U-14+** 1. Feet 250 Times Juggle the ball with your feet 250 times in a row. Feet Only. 2. Thighs 100 Times Juggle the ball with your thighs 100 times in a row. 3. Head 50 Times Juggle the ball with your head 50 times in a row. 4. Juggle the ball over and behind head, repeat until you execute 4 times in a row. Use both feet. 6. Head – Shoulder –Head 6x. Juggle the ball with your head, shoulder, head for 6 touches. 7. 3/4 Around-the-World. Sequence: Right foot, right thigh, head, left thigh, left foot. Repeat going the opposite direction. 8. 5 Small Juggles L & R, 5 small juggles with the right foot. Repeat with the left foot. 9. Hold Ball on Foot for 10 Sec. Pick up ball with foot and balance without ball resting on foot for 10 sec. Repeat with opposite foot. Then do the same from juggling to stalling the ball on your foot.					
TUESDAY If No Team Training Perform the following 6.12	**Beginners U-11 to U-12** 1. Free Juggling 50 Times. Juggle the ball with your feet, thigh and head 50 times in a row. 2. Thighs 25 Times Juggle the ball with your thighs 25 times in a row. 3. Head 10 Times Juggle the ball with your head 10 times in a row. 4. 2 Left and 2 Right with Feet x6. Juggle the ball with your left foot 2 times in a row then your right foot 2 times in a row. Continue until you reach 6 times without dropping ball or 24 touches. 5. 2 Head, Shoulder Juggle the ball twice with your head then your shoulder and back up to your head twice and catch. 6. ½ Around-the-World x5 Right foot, right thigh, left thigh, left foot. Continue around 5 times. **Advanced U-14+** 1. 360° Juggle the ball in a full circle in 7 touches. Once complete, turn the other way. 2. Full Around-the-World. Right foot, right thigh, right shoulder, head, left shoulder, left thigh, left foot. Repeat the opposite way. 3. Spinning Ball Put inside spin on ball with feet for 5 touches in a row, repeat with other foot. Put outside spin on ball with feet for 5 touches in a row, repeat with other foot. 4. No Spin Juggling Juggle with both feet without any spin on the ball. 5. Around-the-Foot While juggling with feet, move foot around the ball while ball is in the air and continue to juggle. 6. 20 Yards in Air - Foot – Thigh – Head. Punt ball 20 yards in air, then foot, then thigh, then head, repeat. 7. 25 Small Juggles L & R 25 small juggles with the right foot. Repeat with the left foot. 8. Juggle on the Move, walking with your feet for 60 yards with out dropping. 9. Juggle on the Move, jogging with your feet for 60 yards with out dropping.					
WEDNESDAY If No Team Training Perform the following 6.13	**Advanced Juggling—The Skill Triangle** Using your feet get the ball into the air at cone 1. 3 Circuit Variations: 1. Juggle with your feet all the way around the triangle. 2. Juggle using your feet and thighs going around the triangle. 3. Full Skill Triangle—Juggling to cone 2 with using your feet only. From cone 2-3 juggle using your thighs. From 3 Back to 1 use your head or shoulders. Try and complete as many circuits as possible.					
THURSDAY If No Team Training Perform the following 6.14	**Advanced Juggling—Slalom Juggling** Arrange 5 cones in a line. At cone (A) get the ball into the air using your feet, then attempt the following activities; 1. Juggle in & out the cones using your feet. 2. Juggle in & out the cones using your right foot/left foot only. 3. Juggle in & out the cones using a combination of feet/thigh/head. Perform 30 attempts at any of the above activities (1-3). (Dribbling on the way back).					
FRIDAY	Free juggling for 20 minutes. Using feet, thigh, shoulder and head.					
SATURDAY	**GAME** OR **REST**					
SUNDAY	**GAME** OR **REST**					

"Players in all positions need to have the ability to receive and control the ball in limited space. The training focus for this week is on 'touch' (the ability to control and receive the ball). When doing juggling practice try to make the targets listed for that day for your age group. Set personal targets to meet each time you do the activity. **Keep working at them and you will improve!!**"

Personal Skill Routine 6.2
☐ CODE YELLOW

Touch & Dribbling

**Parent/Guardian Signature
AND Player Signature**

MONDAY					
If No Team Training Perform the following 6.21	**Dribbling Grid** Set up a 10x10m square with one cone in the middle of the Square. Dribble around the cones in any sequence you like making sure to include runs around the inside cone from time to time. Make sure to use both your feet when dribbling. Each rep should consist of 45 seconds of continuous dribbling. Rest should be 2 minutes. Perform 5 reps.				
TUESDAY					
If No Team Training Perform the following 6.22	**Dribbling Slalom** Set up the cones in a slalom formation as shown on the right. 5 cones should be approximately 5m apart. You can increase or decrease the number of cones in the slalom. Dribble from one end of the slalom to the other performing turns when you get to one of the cones. Try and cut (turn) hard at the cone and accelerate towards the next cone and repeat. Vary you turns from go to go. Rest for 45 seconds after each repetition. Perform the slalom 10 times.				
WEDNESDAY					
If No Team Training Perform the following 6.23	**Wall Ball Work (Wally)** You can use this activity using a wall or a person feeding the ball back to you. Set up 1 cone 4m away from the Wall. Start from one side of the cone and play an angled pass against the wall so that it bounces off to the other side of the cone. Then repeat back from the other side using the other foot. Perform 10 from each side of the cone. Variations: 1. Use a control touch and then pass using left foot on left side and right foot on the right side of the cone. 2. Chip the ball against the wall, you may have to use aerial control when receiving on the other side of the cone. Repeat from other side. 3. Start with a bouncing ball and volley against the wall, control on the other side of the cone, keep the ball bouncing and volley back again, repeat.				
THURSDAY					
If No Team Training Perform the following 6.24	**Juggling + Aerial Control** Juggle the ball freely. After a period of time and when you have the ball under good control kick the ball higher in the air (3-5m). Run and get under the ball and bring the ball down using the following techniques: 1. Feet (Try with both) 2. Thigh (control the ball with your thigh) 3. Chest (control the ball with your chest) 4. Head (attempt to cushion the ball with your head) After each control touch continue juggling, if you need to let the Ball bounce to start with this is fine also.				
FRIDAY 6.25	Free juggling for 20 minutes.				
SATURDAY	**GAME** OR **REST**				
SUNDAY	**GAME** OR **REST**				

"The training focus for this week is on '**touch**' (the ability to control and receive the ball) and dribbling. Every player in all playing positions need to be comfortable dribbling in tight spaces. Good touch is something you need to work on no matter what age you are."

Football Nutrition

Good nutrition and diet is the foundation for physical performance and one of the most important variables in developing a high level of fitness and performance. Food and drink fuels our various energy systems. What you eat and when you eat it can have a significant impact on the outcome of their energy, effort and ability to stay focused during competition.

The foods that we choose before, during and after training and competition will affect how well we play and train and also how quickly we recover. All players should have a nutritional strategy and be aware of how your diet affects your performance and helps you recover. These are the three key areas we can use nutrition (food & drink) to help us:

1. **Optimal Performance in Games and Practices.**
2. **Enhance Recovery from soccer activity.**
3. **Reduced risk of injury and illness.**

Preparation for Competition
You need to rest, sleep and eat well balanced diets during the days prior to an important game or tournament. Below we are going to try and answer some common questions on how much to eat, what type of food and when is the best time to eat.

The Week Before
Carbohydrate is the key energy-providing nutrient that must be optimized during the days leading up to and including the day of competition. Also, you need to be optimizing water and salt levels in the body. Players do not need to increase levels of fat or protein intake above normal training levels. Players who are competing intensely may benefit from 'carbohydrate-loading' for a

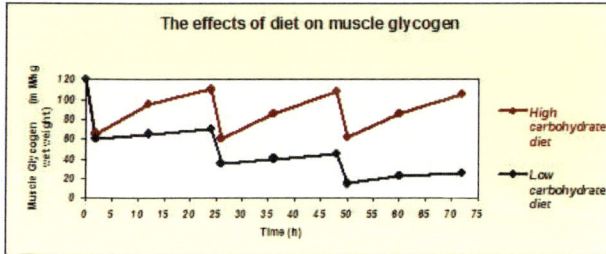

The effects of diet on muscle glycogen

Cosill, D.L., Miller, J.M. Nutrition for endurance sport: Carbohydrate and fluid balance. Int. J. Sport. Med. 1:2-14, 1980.

few days. This loading of muscle glycogen to super-compensate can be achieved within 2-3 days by consuming a large amount of carbohydrate (8-10g per/kg of body weight per day). The graph shows the effects of a player who carbo-loaded (red) and one who did not (black). The carbo loading player had more muscle glycogen (energy fuel) in their muscle after repeated sprints. A good example of a carbo-loading diet is shown in 'Menu 1'.

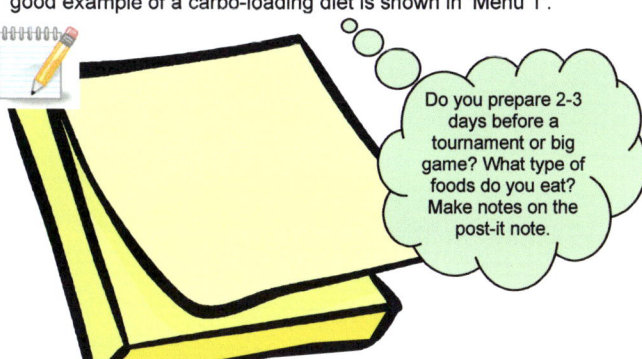

Do you prepare 2-3 days before a tournament or big game? What type of foods do you eat? Make notes on the post-it note.

If your energy sources are low or you have depleted them through long-term activity, your body experiences muscle fatigue. As a competitive soccer player, muscle fatigue results in less shots on goal and poor decision making abilities by allowing muscle memory to slide, and strength to be lost.

MENU 1

Situation: 2-3 days prior.
Example of one day of carbohydrate loading diet providing over 600g of carbohydrate *(i.e. to provide 9g/kg carbs for player weighing 70kg)

Breakfast -
- 2 cups of cereal with Milk (Raison Bran, Cornflakes with milk.)
- 1 cup of fruit
- 1 glass of fruit juice (250ml)
- 1 banana
- 2 thick slices of toast + jam

Snack 1 -
- 1 soft drink (500ml) OR
- 1sports drink (750ml)

Lunch -
- 1 large bread roll sandwich
- 1 medium muffin
- 1 fruit smoothie

Training or PTL -
- Frozen Grapes
- Trail Mix
- 1 Nutrition bar

Immediately After Training or PTL -
- Gatorade
- Banana
- Watermelon
- 1 Confectionery bar (Mars bar, Snicker's, etc)
- Jam (jelly) sandwich (2 slices bread + 2 tbsp. jam)

Dinner -
- 3 cups of cooked pasta
- 1 fruit salad
- 2 scoops of ice-cream
- 1 sports drink (500ml)

Snack 2 (Post Game) -
- 1 cup of fruit
- 1 glass milk

Are these the type of foods you eat 2-3 days before a game?

Daily Snacks

Post Training Snack

High Carb Meals

"Eating a high carbohydrate diet up to the day of competition might help you last longer in the game!"

Eat More
The main fundamental difference in diet between what a player and non-player (non-athlete) eats is volume. Especially if training is continued right up to competition the player should be constantly renewing their energy supplies.

Sample Menus for a soccer player

Shown below are two sample days of the soccer meal strategies with suggested meal plans for you to view. The goal is to space meals every couple of hours apart, combine carbs, proteins and fats at each sitting and provide a variety with foods which focus on healthful choices. The diet commonly recommended for athletes is shown below, and is very close to the regular Recommended Daily Allowance (RDA) Guidelines.

- **65%(+) Carbohydrates**
- **20-25% Fat**
- **10-15% Protein**
- **Lots of Hydration**

Pre-Game meal (3-4hrs before)

Carbohydrates with **low to moderate GI** should be consumed before exercise to slowly raise and maintain energy (blood glucose) levels during the exercise. It is best to select foods that also do not cause stomach cramps or gastrointestinal disturbances, (avoid high fibre and diary products). Refer to the GI chart on page 27 for examples of high and low GI foods. Refer to Menu 2.

Pre-Game Snack (1hr—30mins before)

If only 1 hour remains before the game only water and fluid replacement beverages are recommended such as Gatorade, etc. Eat a high carbohydrate meal (Snack) 1 hr to 30 minutes prior to a game or practice. These high carbohydrate pre-exercise meals improve running capacity. Immediately prior to exercising (5-60 minutes) it is advisable to top up the glycogen (energy) stores by taking in high GI foods.

During Training and Matches

If you are training/playing for more than 60-90 minutes, well-formulated Carbohydrate-electrolyte drinks (i.e. Gatorade) or other forms of carbohydrate (High GI foods) should also be ingested throughout exercise and may help prevent fatigue. Small quantities (150ml) at 20 minute intervals will help to sustain high-intensity exercise. You should be aiming to consume 1g of carbohydrate for every Kg of body weight. For a 50Kg athlete this would be 50g of carbohydrate. Try and calculate it for yourself. **Always remember to drink water** (it re-hydrates you better than any sports-drink!)

Recovery (post game):

The best time to start refueling is as soon as possible after a match or practice, as glycogen storage is faster during the **2 hours** immediately afterwards. Recovery is improved when 50g carbohydrate is consumed immediately after prolonged exercise (a game) and at 1hr intervals thereafter. Aim to eat **High GI foods**, at least 1g carbohydrate per Kg of body weight at 1-hour intervals during the 4-hour period following exercise. At 80g carbohydrate: (e.g. ½ pint isotonic drink and 1 banana). Even if you don't feel like eating try and eat something.

Here are some quick high carbohydrate energy football snacks that have been recommended by nutritional experts.

FOOTBALL SNACKS - SUSTAINED ENERGY!

Examples of foods as PRE OR POST GAME snacks:

- ½ Whole Wheat Bagel with Lean Turkey Slices
- Applesauce or Low fat Yogurt
- Protein Bar with Sliced Apples
- Trail Mix
- Sliced Pear or Apple
- Veggie Wrap with Avocado
- Banana with Peanut Butter
- Frozen (or unfrozen) Grapes
- Veggie Wrap with Almonds
- Balance Bar or similar protein bar
- Baked Potato
- Macaroni & Cheese

Pre-Game Meal (3-4 hrs before)

Recovery Snack (Post game)

MENU 2

Situation: Game at 1.30pm

Breakfast -
- 2 slices of whole wheat toast with peanut butter
- 1 cup of oatmeal with 1 cup of lowfat/nonfat milk
- 1 banana
- 1 cup of orange juice

Snack 1 -
- 4 oz cottage cheese
- 1/2 cup peaches
- 1 glass milk

Lunch-
- 1 Turkey Sandwich on whole grain bread
- 1 cup of vegetable soup
- 1 cup of fresh fruit salad

Pre & During Game-
- Frozen Grapes
- Trail Mix
- 1 Nutrition bar

Immediately After Game-
- Gatorade
- Banana
- Watermelon
- 1 Confectionary bar (Mars bar, Snicker's, etc)
- Jam (jelly) sandwich (2 slices bread with jam)

Snack 2 (Post Game) -
- 1 nutrition bar
- 16 ounces of apple juice

- 1/2 cup peaches
- 1 glass milk

Dinner -
- 6 ounces of grilled chicken breast
- 1 cup of pasta/tomato sauce
- 1 cup of steamed green beans
- 1 cup of low fat/non-fat milk

Players need to adjust the values above to suit their age and size.

MENU 3

Situation: Game at 9am & 4pm

Breakfast -
- 2 eggs and/ or egg whites (with vegetables)
- 1 slice of whole wheat toast
- 1 banana
- 1 cup of orange juice

Pre & During Game-
- Frozen Grapes
- Trail Mix
- 1 Nutrition bar

Immediately After Game-
- Gatorade
- Banana
- Watermelon

Lunch-
- 1 wheat tortilla
- 1 ounce of chicken
- 1 cup salad with salsa

During Game Snacks

Snack 1 -
- Sliced Apple or Pear
- 1 Granola bar

Pre & During Game-
- Frozen Grapes
- Trail Mix
- 1 Nutrition bar

Immediately After Game-
- Gatorade
- Banana
- Watermelon
- 1 Confectionary bar (Mars bar, Snicker's, etc)
- Jam (jelly) sandwich

Snack 2 (Post Game) -
- 2 Mozzarella cheese sticks
- 1/2 cup fruit
- 1 glass milk

Dinner -
- 6 ounces of grilled chicken breast
- 1 cup of rice
- 2 vegetables
- 2 cups of low-fat/non-fat milk

Recovery Meal (post game)

SOCCER MEAL PLANNER!

Your dietary intake is an important factor in your performance and ability to compete both physically and mentally. You may have a demanding schedule of training and traveling, coupled with a possible lack of nutritional knowledge, which may prohibit you from maintaining your optimal dietary intake. As part of a good training program you need to monitor your diet to reach peak performance.

Based on what you now know from pages 25-26 about when and what to eat around your soccer week you can start to use the chart below to customize your own soccer meals! The chart over the page also shows how it is important to eat the right foods to peak at the right time.

THE 'GI FACTOR' AND SOCCER PERFORMANCE

HIGH (60-100)	GI	MODERATE (40-60)	GI	LOW (<40)	GI
Breakfast Cereals		**Breakfast Cereals**		**Breakfast Cereals**	
Nutri-grain	66	All-bran	42	Rice Bran	19
Shredded Wheat	69	Porridge (oatmeal)	49	Kellogg's' All Bran Fruit 'n	39
Golden Grahams	71	Bran Buds	53	Oats	46
Puffed Wheat	74	Special K	54		
Cheerios	74	Kellogg's' Honey Smacks	55		
Wheatabix	75	Muesli	56		
Kellogg's' Breakfast Bar	76	Kellogg's' Just Right	59		
Rice Krispies	82				
Cornflakes	83				
Crispix	87				
Cereal Grains		**Cereal Grains**		**Cereal Grains**	
Couscous	65	Oats	49	Barley	22
White bread	69	Bulgar wheat	48		
Wholemeal bread	72				
Brown rice	80				
White rice	82				
Fruit		**Fruit**		**Fruit**	
Raisins	64	Apple juice	41	Cherries	22
Pineapple	66	Peach	42	Grapefruit	25
watermelon	72	Orange	44	Apricots, dries	31
		Pear, canned	44	Pear, fresh	37
		Grapes	46	Apple	38
		Pineapple juice	46	Plum	39
		Orange juice	52		
		Banana	54		
		Sultanas	56		
Vegetables		**Vegetables**		**Dairy products**	
Potato, mashed	71	White potato, boiled	59	Yogurt, low fat, artificially	27
French fries	75	Yam	51	Milk, full fat	32
Potato, baked	90	Sweet potato	51	Milk, skimmed	33
parsnips	97	Crisps	51	Yogurt, low fat, fruit, sugar	37
		Sweet corn	55		
		Peas	48		
Others		**Others**		**Others**	
Muesli bars	61	Oatmeal cookies	55	Peanuts	15
Shortbread biscuit	64	Digestives	59	Mars M&Ms (peanut)	32
Mars bar	64	Other cont.	40	Other cont.	32
Arrowroot biscuit	69	Mars Snickers bar	49	Fettuccine	35
Mars Skittles	71	Jams and marmalades	54	Vermicelli	37
Water crackers	77	Chocolate	55	Spaghetti, whole meal	39
Rice cakes	79	Honey	54		
Morning coffee biscuit	72	Spaghetti, white	41		
Macaroni and cheese	69	Macaroni	45		

The **Glycemic Index (GI)** of a food refers to how quickly the food is turned into glucose in the blood stream where it can be used by your muscles.

How quickly the blood sugar rises and falls varies with different foods as you can see in the chart.

A low GI food will raise the blood sugar slowly, while a high GI food will give a fast rise in the blood sugar and therefore a quicker availability of energy. **Low GI foods** are digested slowly and can remain in your stomach for hours after consumption (so can't be eaten close to game time!).

There are times when low GI foods provide an advantage and times when high GI foods are better. **High GI foods** release their glucose (energy) quickly and can be eaten closer to game/practice time. They are digested a lot quicker!" The summary section below highlights when low GI foods should be eaten and when high GI foods should be eaten.

Remember the following rules when planning your own custom soccer meal:

✓ **Low GI foods** are good *slow release* energy foods and should be taken in the build up to exercise 3-4 hours prior to a game or practice.

✓ **High GI foods** are good *fast release* energy foods and should be taken in the 30 minutes prior to exercise (game or practice) and during exercise (half time, extra time).

"When planning to eat before/after and during training and games take note of the above. My pre-game (30mins to 1hr before) snack favorites are highlighted in Red. Green indicates some of my favorite pre-match meals (3-4hrs before the game). and Black is highest GI values. If you eat the wrong things you are not helping yourself play to your full potential. Worse still you could end up with stomach cramps or dehydration which could affect your performance by over 10%!!)."

Eating to Peak at the right Time!

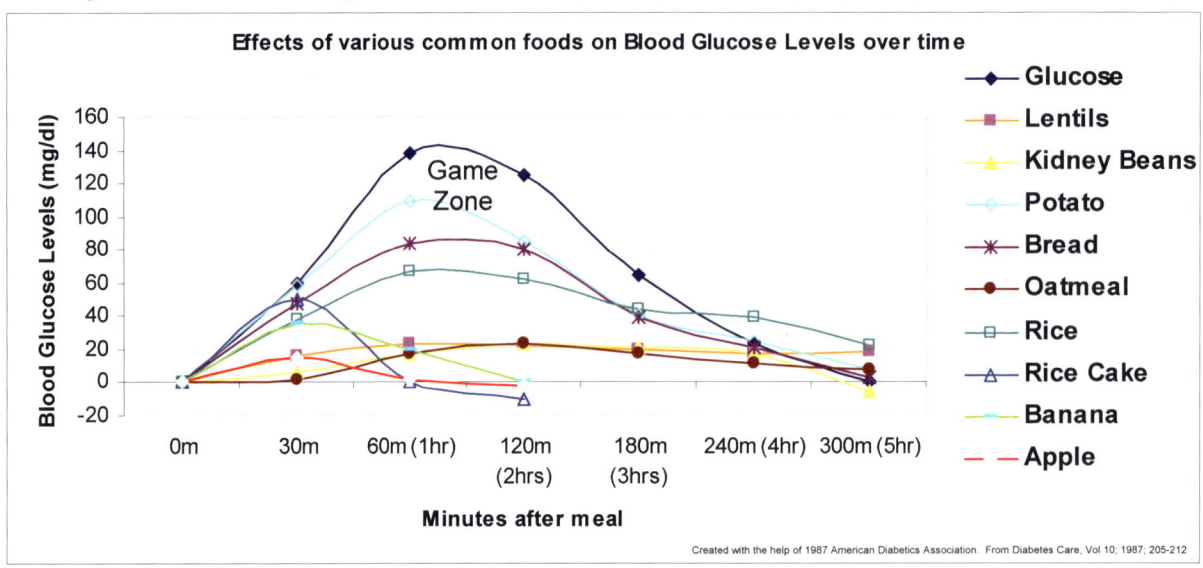

Effects of various common foods on Blood Glucose Levels over time

Legend: Glucose, Lentils, Kidney Beans, Potato, Bread, Oatmeal, Rice, Rice Cake, Banana, Apple

Blood Glucose Levels (mg/dl) — Game Zone — Minutes after meal

Created with the help of 1987 American Diabetics Association. From Diabetes Care, Vol 10; 1987; 205-212

Remember High and Low GI foods peak at different times. DON'T EAT HIGH GI FOODS 2-3 HRS BEFORE.

 CAUTION: Consumption of high GI foods should be limited to immediately before or during practice or a game to avoid hypoglycemia. Notice how High GI foods spike and cause a rapid decline in blood glucose levels (Rice Cake for example). Remember the duration of a soccer game is usually between 60-90 minutes. Try and make good food selections so that you maintain energy throughout a game and peak at the right times. Notice for the selection of foods selected in the graph above most of them provide optimal levels 1 hr after the meal.

Choose Wisely

The chart above shows how various food types affect the muscle glucose (energy) level in our muscles. The GI table on the previous page will help you to determine between high GI and low GI foods. It is essential to have a wide range of low GI carbs to maintain energy in tournaments and other multi-game schedules. Use the table on page 27 and the chart above to select the right types of foods to eat at the right times.

Fluids

Fluid consumption plays a huge role in helping us before, during and after games and practices for optimal performance and good health. They transport the Glucose to our muscles and transport the waste products away. They help us sweat which keeps us for overheating. They also help us digest our food.

Players need to drink sufficient fluids with meals on the day before competition to ensure they are well hydrated for competition.

60-90 mins Before Game –
[IF HOT DAY] 500ml in this period before the game.

15 mins Before Game - 300-600ml of fluid.

During Game - Water and carbohydrate sports drinks (Gatorade) Appox. 200ml or whatever the player is comfortable with. With a carbohydrate content of 4-8%.

Summary

√ **High carbohydrate, pre-exercise meals improve exercise capacity. (1-3 hrs prior)**
√ **Carbohydrate-electrolyte drinks (Gatorade) ingested immediately before and during exercise are beneficial.**
√ **Consume low GI foods in game day pre-meals to allow for sustained energy release during a game or practice. Low GI meals should be 2-3 hours before kick-off.**
√ **Try and eat High GI foods immediately after a game or practice, as this will allow you to refuel and recover faster before your next training session or game.**
√ **Fluid ingestion during prolonged exercise helps delay the deterioration of your skills.**
√ **During training or matches, recovery is likely to be improved when carbohydrate intake is increased.**
√ **Re-hydration is quickly achieved during recovery when athletes ingest fluids.**
In hot weather, water intake needs to increase.